The Classic Guitar Collection. Volume One.

Edited and transcribed by Harvey Vinson.
This album was formerly distributed under the title
'Music For Classic Guitar', Music for Millions Series Volume 59.

AMSCO
NEW YORK · LONDON · SYDNEY

Published 1977 by
Amsco Music Publishing Company
(A division of Music Sales Limited,
8/9 Frith Street, London W1V 5TZ.)
London/New York/Sydney

Cover illustration by Adrian George
Designed by Pearce Marchbank

Exclusive distributors:
Music Sales Limited,
8/9 Frith Street,
London W1V 5TZ,
England.
Music Sales Corporation,
257 Park Avenue South,
New York,
NY 10010,
U.S.A.
Music Sales Pty. Limited,
120 Rothschild Avenue,
Rosebery, NSW 2018,
Australia.

Amsco Music Publishing Company

U.K. ISBN 0.86001.451.7   U.S.A. ISBN 0.8256.2268.9
U.K. Order No. AM 32657   U.S.A. Order No. 020268.9

Anonymous
Estampe, 4

Anonymous
Nachtanz, 6
Tedesca, 6

Anonymous
Dance, 15
Greensleeves, 7
Italiana, 14
Passamezzo, 7
Song, 14

Galilei, Vincenzo
Saltarello, 8

Milan, Luis
Pavana, 11

Morlaye, G.
Galliard, 12

Narváez, Luys de
Y La Mi Cinta Dorada, 13

Newsidler, Hans
Dance of the Washerwomen, 9
Hapfauf, 10

Terzi, Antonio
Allemande, 12

Besardo, Giovanni
Branle, 24

Dowland, John
Mistress Winter's Jump, 16

Roncalli, Lodovíco
Sarabande, 16

Sanz, Gaspar
Eight Easy Dances, 17
Spanish Dance, 20

Visée, Robert de
Minuet in D, 23
Passacaille, 22

Bach, Johann Sebastian
Gavotte, 24

Aguado, Dionisio
Adagio in E Minor, 82
Adagio in G, 86
Andante in A Minor, 81
Andante in C, 83
Andante in D, 84
Andante in E Minor, 84
Andante in G, 86

Anonymous
Romanza, 68

Diabelli, Antonio
Minuet in C, 78
Minuet in F, 80
Moderato in D, 80

Carcassi, Matteo
Six Easy Preludes, 87
Andantino in C, 90
Andantino in G, 90
Song, 92

Carulli, Ferdinando
Allegro in A Minor, 27

Capriccio in C, 38
Caprice in G, 25
Lento in E Minor, 31
Prelude in C, 26
Prelude in G, 26
Prelude in A Minor, 29
Prelude in A, 32
Prelude in D Minor, 34
Prelude in E Minor, 36
Prelude in A Minor, 37
Waltz in A, 25
Waltz in G, 28
Waltz in G, 30
Waltz in E, 35
Waltz and Variations, 32

Giuliani, Mauro
Four Northern Dances, Op. 14, 72
Allegro in A, 72
Andantino in C, 77
Andante in C, 70

Küffner, Joseph
Allegro Moderato in C, 45
Four Easy Pieces, 43
Ländler, 44
Theme and Variations, 45

Kunz, Konrad
Two Short Canons, 67

Meignen, L.
Waltz, 68

Sor, Fernando
Allegretto in C, 50
Allegretto Moderato in D, 56
Allegro in C, 49
Allegro in G, 53
Allegro in C, 62
Allegro in C, 63
Andante in C, 48
Andante in G, 50
Andante in C, 51
Andante in C, 54
Andante in C, 55
Andante in A, 58
Andante in E Minor, 64
Andantino in C, 60
Andantino in E Minor, 66
Lento in A, 59
Moderato in C, 48
Moderato in C, 52
Moderato in C, 53
Moderato in C, 54
Moderato in E Minor, 57
Moderato in A Minor, 58
Moderato in A Minor, 60
Moderato in C, 61
Moderato in D, 65

Bártok, Béla
Two Miniatures, 95

Tárrega, Francisco
Adagio in A, 93
Adelita (Mazurka), 93
Lagrima (Prelude), 94

Estampe.

Anonymous
(14th century)

Tedesca.

Anonymous
(15th Century)

Moderato

*This dance and the following dance, the *Nachtanz* (after-dance) are paired dances and can be played together.

Nachtanz.

Anonymous
(15th Century)

Allegro

Greensleeves.

Anonymous
(16th Century)

Passamezzo.

Anonymous
(16th Century)

* Tune 6th string (lowest in pitch) down to D, an octave lower than the 4th string.

Saltarello.

⑥ = D

＊Vincenzo Galilei
(16th Century)

＊Father of the Italian astronomer, Galileo.
＊＊Tune 6th string down to D, an octave lower than the 4th string.

Dance of the Washerwomen.

Moderato

Hans Newsidler
(16th Century)

Hapfauf.

Hans Newsidler

* The *Haupfauf* ("jumping dance") should be played immediately
after the *Dance of the Washerwomen* The tradition of coupling
slow dances in duple meter to quicker ones in triple meter was
quite common in the 16th century.

Pavana.

Luis Milan
(C. 1500–1561)

Allemande.

Antonio Terzi
(16th Century)

Maestoso

Galliard.

G. Morlaye
(16th Century)

12

Y La Mi Cinta Dorada.

Luys de Narvaéz
(16th Century)

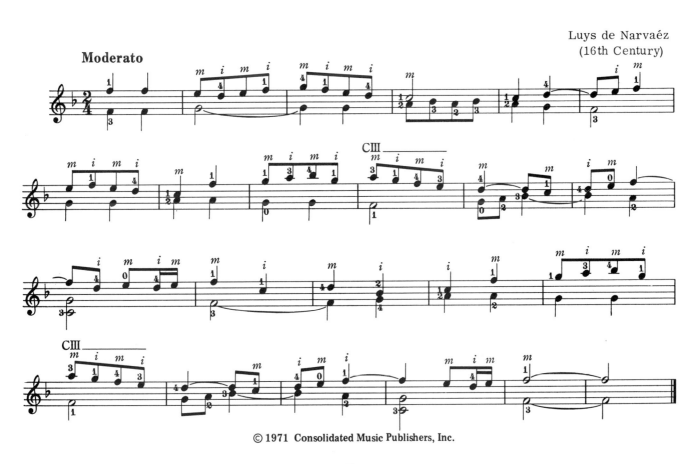

Italiana.

Anonymous
(16th Century)

Song.

Anonymous
(16th Century)

14

Dance.

Anonymous
(16th Century)

*Tune 6th string down to D, an octave lower than the 4th string.

Mistress Winter's Jump.

Allegro

John Dowland
(1562–1626)

Sarabande.

Andantino

Lodovíco Roncalli
(17th Century)

Eight Easy Dances.

1) Mariona

Gaspar Sanz
(17th Century)

2) Dance de las Hachas

3) Españoleta

4) Pavana

Moderato

5) Gallarda

Allegro

6) Villano

7) Iorneo

8) Batalla

Spanish Dance.

Gaspar Sanz

D.C. al Fine

Passacaille.

Robert de Visée
(17th Century)

Minuet in D.

Andante

Robert de Visée

Branle.

Giovanni Besardo
(17th Century)

Gavotte.

Johann Sebastian Bach
(1685–1750)

*Tune 6th string down to D, an octave lower than the 4th string.

Caprice in G.

Ferdinando Carulli
(1770–1841)

Waltz in A.

Ferdinando Carulli

Prelude in C.

Allegro

Ferdinando Carulli

Prelude in G.

Allegro

Ferdinando Carulli

Allegro in A Minor.

Ferdinando Carulli

Waltz in G.

Ferdinando Carulli

Prelude in A Minor.

Moderato

Ferdinando Carulli

Waltz in G.

Ferdinando Carulli

Lento in E Minor.

Ferdinando Carulli

Prelude in A.

Moderato

Ferdinando Carulli

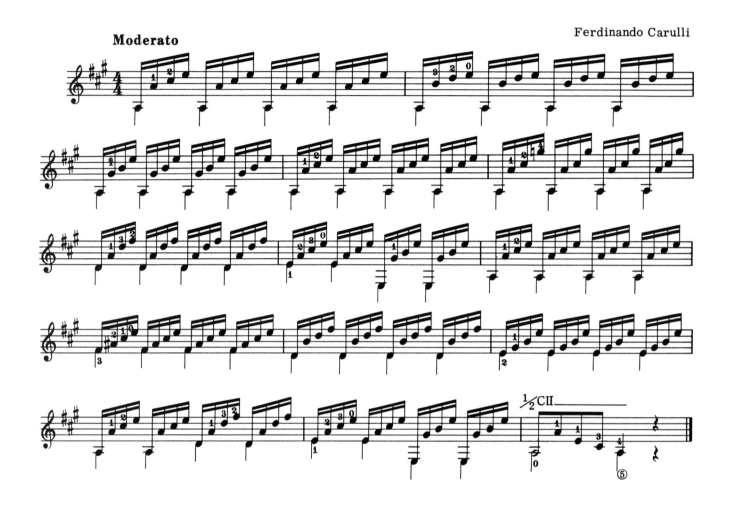

Waltz and Variations.

Allegro

Ferdinando Carulli

Fine

D.C. al Fine

33

Prelude in D Minor.

Allegro

Ferdinando Carulli

Waltz in E.

Ferdinando Carulli

Prelude in E Minor.

Ferdinando Carulli

Prelude in A Minor.

Moderato

Ferdinando Carulli

Capriccio in C.

Ferdinando Carulli

Moderato

Vivace

41

42

Four Easy Pieces.

Joseph Küffner
(1776–1856)

1) Andantino

2) Andantino

3) Andantino

4) Andante

Ländler.

Moderato

Joseph Küffner

Allegro Moderato in C.

Joseph Küffner

Theme and Variations.

Andante

Joseph Küffner

Var. I

Var. II

46

Var. III

Andante in C.

Fernando Sor
(1778-1839)

Moderato in C.

Fernando Sor

Allegro in C.

Fernando Sor

Andante in G.

Fernando Sor

Allegretto in C.

Fernando Sor

Andante in C.

Fernando Sor

Moderato in C.

Fernando Sor

Moderato in C.

Fernando Sor

Allegro in G.

Fernando Sor

Moderato in C.

Fernando Sor

D.C. al Fine

Andante in C.

Fernando Sor

Andante in C.

Fernando Sor

Allegretto Moderato in D.

Fernando Sor

Moderato in E Minor.

Fernando Sor

Moderato in A Minor.

Fernando Sor

Andante in A.

Fernando Sor

Lento in A.

Fernando Sor

Andantino in C.

Fernando Sor

Moderato in A Minor.

Fernando Sor

Moderato in C.

Fernando Sor

Allegro in C.

Fernando Sor

Allegro in C.

Fernando Sor

Andante in E Minor.

Fernando Sor

Moderato in D.

*⑥ = D

Fernando Sor

Tune 6th string (lowest in pitch) down to D, an octave lower than the 4th string.

Andantino in E Minor.

Fernando Sor

Two Short Canons.

Konrad Kunz
(19th Century)

1) **Allegretto**

2) **Moderato**

Waltz.

L. Meignen
(19th Century)

Romanza.

Anonymous
(19th Century)

69

Andante in C.

Mauro Giuliani
(1780 – 1840)

Allegro in A.

Mauro Giuliani

Four Northern Dances, Op. 14.

Mauro Giuliani

1) **Grazioso**

2) **Allegretto**

Trio

3) Allegretto

75

4) Allegro vivace

Andantino in C.

Mauro Giuliani

Minuet in C.

Antonio Diabelli
(1781–1858)

Minuet in F.

Antonio Diabelli

Moderato in D.

Antonio Diabelli

Andante in A Minor.

Dionisio Aguado
(1789–1849)

Adagio in E Minor.

Dionisio Aguado

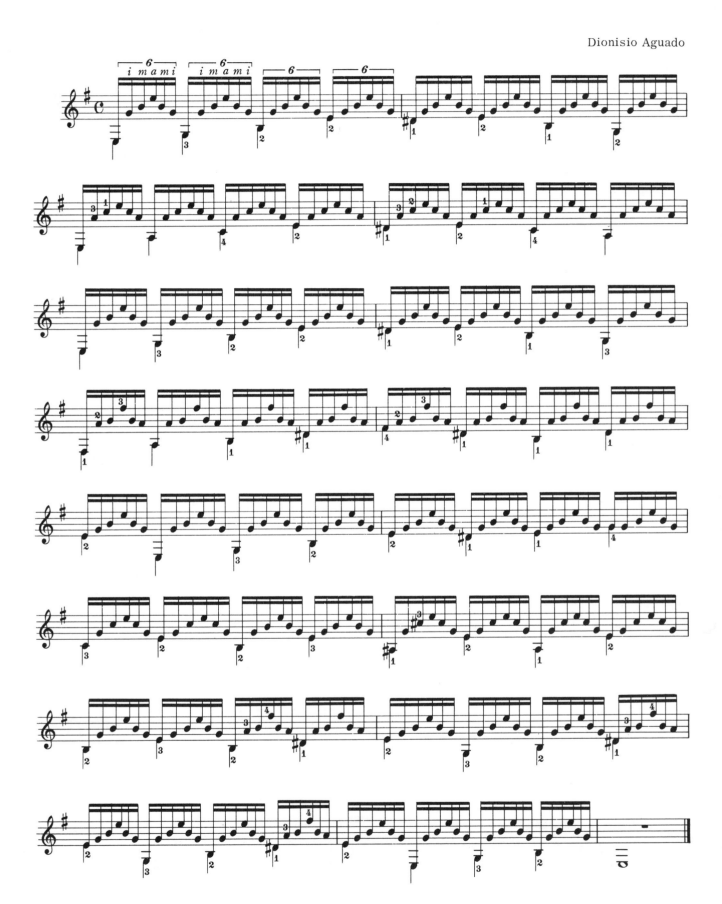

Andante in C.

Dionisio Aguado

Andante in D.

Dionisio Aguado

Andante in E Minor.

Dionisio Aguado

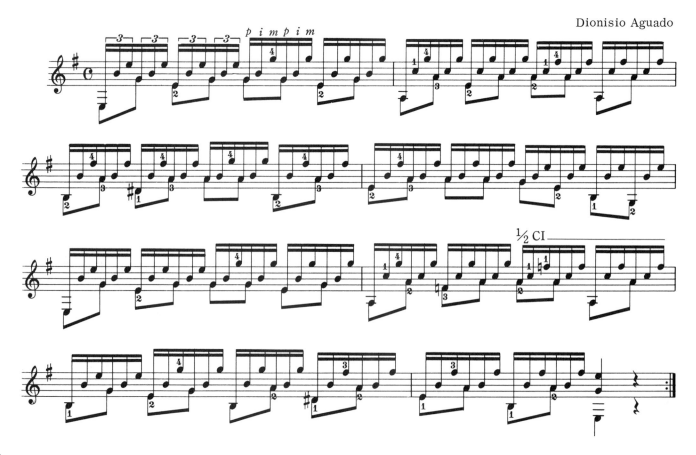

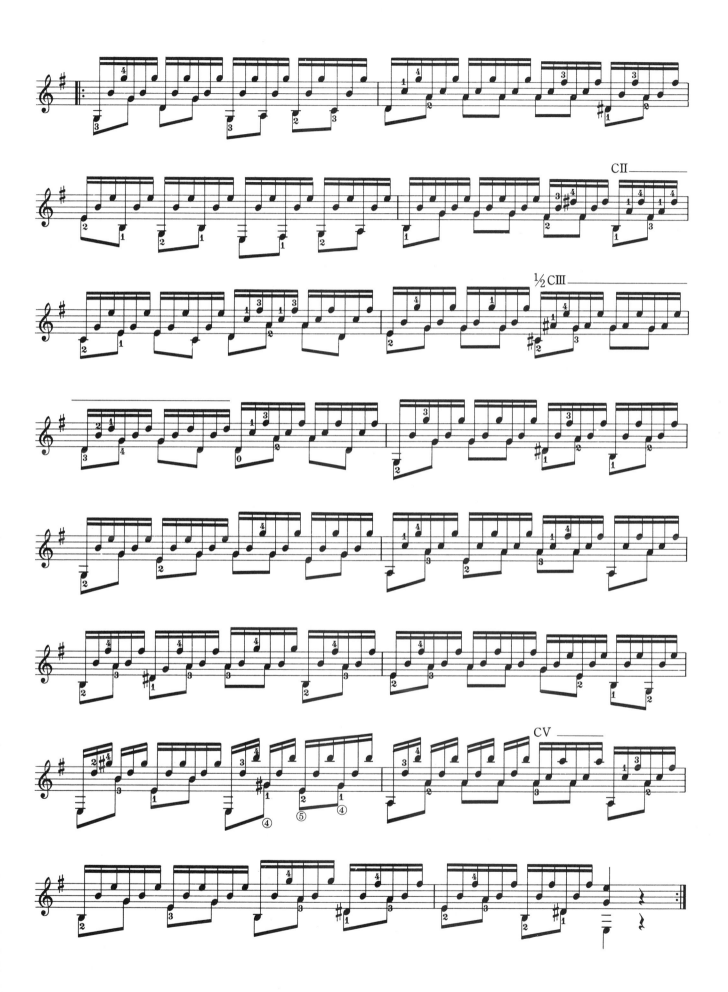

Adagio in G.

Dionisio Aguado

Andante in G.

Dionisio Aguado

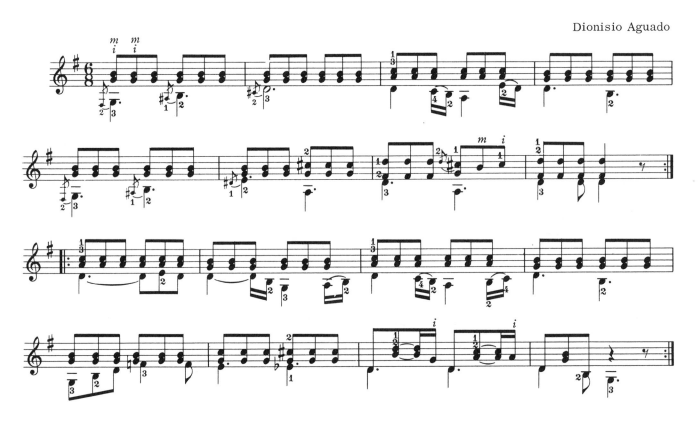

Six Easy Preludes.

Matteo Carcassi
(1792–1853)

6) **Allegro**

Andantino in C.

Matteo Carcassi

Andantino in G.

Matteo Carcassi

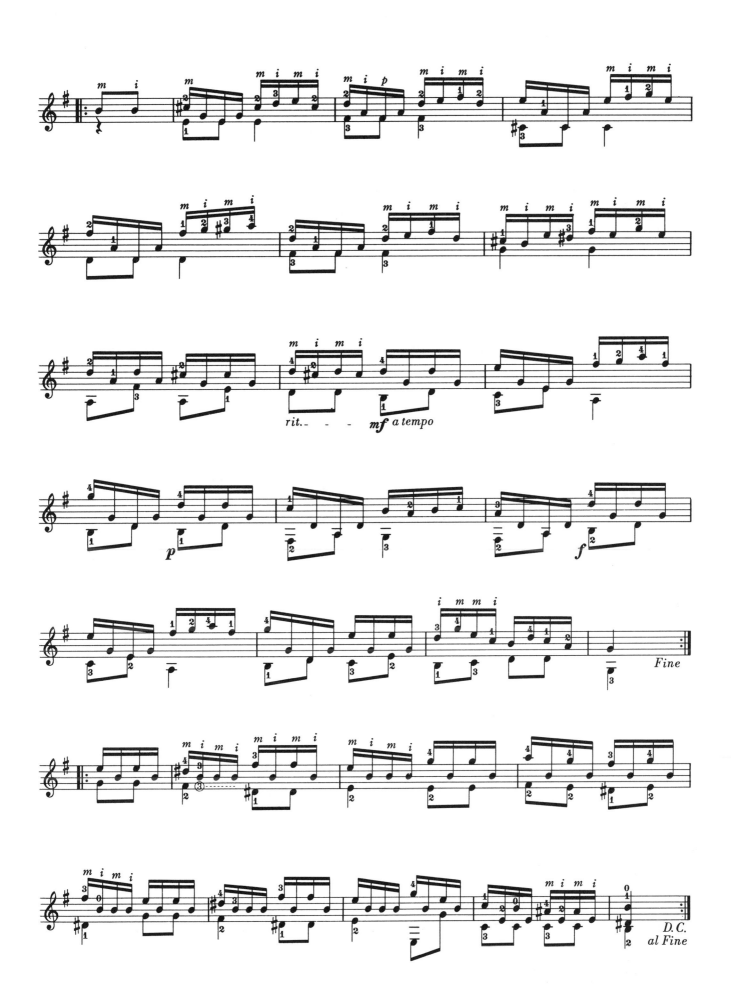

Song.

Matteo Carcassi

Adagio in A.

Francisco Tárrega
(1854–1909)

Adelita (Mazurka).

Francisco Tárrega

Lagrima (Prelude).

Francisco Tárrega

Two Miniatures.

Béla Bartók
(1881–1945)

1) **Allegro**

2) **Largo**

Printed and bound in Great Britain by
Caligraving Limited Thetford Norfolk

6/96 (24408)